8p GUERNSEY

Royal Wedding
EIIR
$3
ANGUILLA

TRACEY ALDERSON

Acknowledgments:

The author and publishers wish to acknowledge the use of photographs and other material as follows: page 24, Broadlands (Romsey) Ltd; front endpaper designed and photographed by Tim Clark; page 6 (both), Eastern Daily Press; pages 11, 12, 13 (both), 19, 20, 22, 27 (both), 28, 33 (top), 37, 39, 40, 41, 43, 44 (top), 45, 46 (both), 47, 48 (both), 50 (both), 51, Fox Photos; cover, title page, pages 4, 5, 7, 9 (top right), 10, 11 (top right), 14, 15, 16, 18, 25 (both), 26, 29, 30, 31 (both), 32, 35, 36, 38, 44 (bottom), 49 (both), and back cover, Tim Graham; family tree and succession table (back endpaper), R M Powell; pages 8, 9 (top left, bottom right), 10 (bottom left), 17, 21 (both), 23, 33 (bottom), 34 (both), Syndication International. The Joint Coat of Arms is reproduced by permission of the Lord Chamberlain's Office.

First Edition

by BRENDA RALPH LEWIS

Ladybird Books Loughborough

The day Prince Charles became engaged to Lady Diana Spencer, 24th February 1981, it was obvious that she fitted very well the demanding recipe for a Princess of Wales and future Queen of England. Charles himself had often said his wife would have to be a 'pretty unusual' person, and Diana turned out to be an uncommon mixture of old-fashioned virtues and modern vivacity. She was homeloving, dutiful, and wanted 'lots and lots' of children; she was discreet and unpretentious, despite her aristocratic background. Yet she also possessed the good looks, charm and outgoing manner the public role of royalty requires.

Her suitability was at once apparent when the engagement ended years of speculation about Charles's future queen. The couple posed for photographers in the gardens behind Buckingham Palace, and Britain welcomed Diana into the royal family without reservation, making her the most popular royal bride anyone can remember.

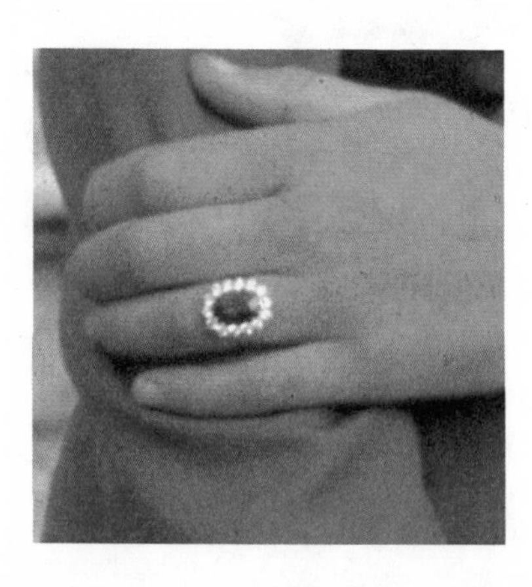

The engagement ring naturally enough was a focus of special attention. A beautiful sapphire circled with diamonds, its cost was said to be £28,000

On the day their engagement was announced, Prince Charles and Lady Diana were photographed together for the first time

Lady Diana and friend – her pet guineapig 'Peanuts'

Lady Diana Spencer was born at Sandringham on 1st July 1961, the third daughter of Earl Spencer and his first wife, formerly the Honourable Frances Roche. The Spencers' long history as advisers and servants to British kings and queens meant that Lady Diana found royalty neither mysterious nor remote. She was, in fact, the girl next door for the Royal Family, for she spent much of her childhood at Park House, on the Queen's Sandringham estate. To her, the Queen was 'Aunt Lilibet', and her childhood chums were the Queen's younger sons, Andrew and Edward. By all accounts they made quite a mischievous crew.

As bridesmaid at her sister's wedding in 1978

Diana's early years were not always so carefree, for her parents were divorced when she was about six. Nevertheless, Diana grew into an uncomplicated teenager with a great sense of fun. Prince Charles later recalled her as 'a splendid sixteen year old' when her elder sister Sarah introduced them to each other in 1977. That year Diana left school, where she was more distinguished for her good nature and love of sports than for her academic achievements. Afterwards, she spent a brief six months at a Swiss finishing school.

Althorp – the Spencer family home

Already, it was clear that a madcap social whirl was not the scene for a girl who loved the countryside, reading, ballet, music and above all, loved young children. It was no surprise to anyone who knew her, therefore, when Diana became a teacher at a kindergarten in Pimlico. And it was there, in November 1980, that the Press began to watch and photograph Lady Diana, after rumours grew that she meant true love at last for the heir to the throne.

'Charles watchers', always on the lookout for his latest romance, were quick to notice when Lady Diana spent the first weekend in September 1980 at Balmoral.

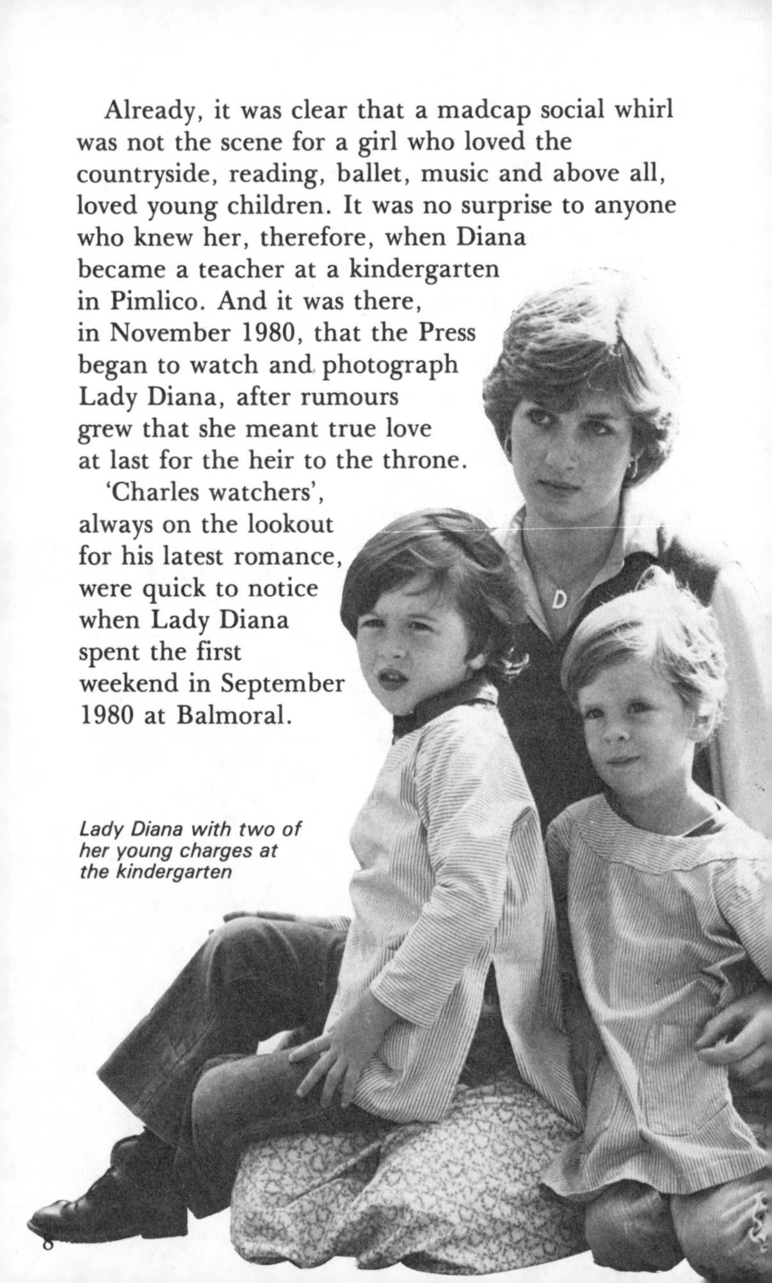

Lady Diana with two of her young charges at the kindergarten

The flat in Earl's Court, London, shared by Lady Diana and two girl friends (above left)

Earl Spencer (above right)

This was not her first holiday with the royal family – she had been with them at Cowes in July – but it soon turned out to be a special one. That weekend, Diana's relationship with Prince Charles deepened as they walked, talked and went fishing together. A bunch of red roses and a telephone call from Charles followed Diana when she returned to London.

A wistful look – before the engagement

The press lay in wait to take pictures such as these . . .

With the Press now alerted, meetings during subsequent weeks involved some cunning. Press speculation grew so much that the Pimlico kindergarten, and Lady Diana, were more or less under siege from reporters and photographers. She had to drop out of a planned skiing holiday because of the publicity.

On his return from that holiday, Charles

Lady Diana was introduced to royal public life on 9th March at a charity show at Goldsmiths Hall in aid of the Royal Opera House Development Fund. She wore a stunning black silk taffeta gown by David and Elizabeth Emmanuel, the designers she chose to make her wedding dress

proposed over a candlelit dinner. But it seemed Diana had no need to 'think things over' during her forthcoming trip to Australia, as Charles suggested. She appeared to have no doubts, and a few days after she came back from Australia, the engagement was announced.

At Ascot in June

Her engagement had a double significance for Lady Diana. She was marrying the man she loved, but she was also, as the future bride of the heir to the throne, saying goodbye to the easygoing private life she had known before. No more popping down to local markets to buy a new sweater or a pair of jeans, or indeed going anywhere on her own. The police assigned to guard her saw to that.

Lady Diana also had to say goodbye to her young charges at the Pimlico kindergarten and to the South Kensington flat which her father had bought for her. As Prince Charles' fiancée, she now came under the protection of the royal family, and she went to live

Royal walkabout at Ascot, with the Queen and the Queen Mother

And an Ascot hat . . .

with the Queen Mother at Clarence House. The pull of royal duty also came home to Diana when on 29th March, Prince Charles left, alone, for a long tour of Australasia. Their parting was described by airport officials as the 'most touching' they had ever seen.

With Princess Margaret at a film première

In tears – overwhelmed by the crowds – a moment that caught the public sympathy

For another official visit on 27th March, Charles and Diana went to Cheltenham Police Headquarters, which provides the guard on Highgrove House. Later that day, at a Cheltenham school, one of the pupils, 18 year old Nicholas Hardy, kissed the hand of his future queen with good oldfashioned gallantry.

Diana had become an instant fashion pacesetter, and her style was closely examined every time she appeared in public in subsequent weeks – at the Sandown Park Races in March, at Ascot in June, at the Wimbledon Tennis Finals in July, and at film premières and art exhibitions. The casual windswept Lady Diana hairstyle was copied in thousands of salons – so much that in Australia, Prince Charles was presented with a bevy of Diana 'lookalikes'. That black silk taffeta dress was copied and in the dress shops within forty-eight hours of being seen, and the fashion conscious were already noting Diana's low-heeled shoes, fondness for feminine frills, choker necklaces and ability to look good in almost any colour.

The Emmanuels' wedding dress however was kept a strict secret. All anyone knew was that when Lady Diana emerged from the final fitting a few days before the wedding, she was said to be delighted.

Leaving St Paul's after the wedding rehearsal

Clementine Hambro, one of the five bridesmaids

The wedding of Prince Charles and Lady Diana Spencer on Wednesday, 29th July 1981, was the most public royal wedding ever – a world-wide event. Some seven hundred million people in fifty countries watched on television.

Viewers watched the processions to St Paul's, the London streets crammed with cheering crowds waving scores of Union Jacks, and every word and expression of the young couple as they took their vows before the Archbishop of Canterbury and their two thousand five hundred wedding guests. Also included among the viewers were dressmakers who sketched Diana's puff-sleeved and lavishly lace-trimmed wedding gown and had the first copy in a London shop within five hours.

World-wide audiences saw the couple's appearance with the royal family on the balcony at Buckingham Palace – including the famous kiss! The five bridesmaids looked enchanting and were very popular, as were the two young pages dressed in naval uniform of the 1860s.

Later the bride and groom left in an open landau for Waterloo station. There they boarded the train that took them to Broadlands for the first three days of their honeymoon.

The delightfully feminine wedding slippers with their heart-shaped decoration – and also the garter, worn for luck

On 5th August, the Monday after the wedding, many of the gifts received by Prince Charles and his new Princess of Wales were put on display to the public at St James's Palace in London.

The focus of special interest was, of course, the Princess's wedding dress and slippers, which were on show together with a bridesmaid's outfit and naval uniform of 1863, worn by the pages.

Some of the really magnificent presents – the crystal bowl is from the President of the United States and his wife

A
Charles

Crowds came to queue in their hundreds to look at the beautiful silver plate, cut glass, sets of cutlery, paintings, statuettes, vases, sculptures, carpets and other presents.

The display, which was in aid of the Royal Wedding Souvenir Fund for the Disabled, made a profit of £86,000 by the time it closed on 4th October.

Later, two hundred presents were put on show at Cardiff, and a further showing was planned at Holyrood House, Edinburgh.

Many of the gifts sent showed how the young couple's tastes and interests had been taken into account

Broadlands

As honeymooners – first at Broadlands, then on their Mediterranean cruise on the royal yacht *Britannia*, and finally back at Balmoral in Scotland, the Prince and Princess of Wales regained for a while the peace and privacy which Diana at least might have thought was a thing of the past. During the cruise in particular, the new Princess was able to see at first hand the techniques of evasion which have been perfected over the years by both the members and the servants of the Royal Family. Prince and Princess succeeded so well in avoiding the prying eyes and cameras of tourists and pressmen that they were photographed only when they wanted to be – first at Gibraltar, then when *Britannia* arrived at Port Said at the entrance to the Suez Canal, next when they posed for pictures with their dinner guests, the Egyptian President Sadat and his English-born wife Jihan, and finally at the airport when they were returning.

A wave from the yacht

Britannia leaving Gibraltar

The honeymoon nevertheless had some unscheduled incidents. Off Sardinia, *Britannia* was involved in the rescue of a British woman whose motor cruiser got into difficulties. Later some Greek photographers planned to break the honeymoon seclusion and overfly *Britannia* in a helicopter. They were however threatened with being shot down if they did so, and smartly cancelled their flight. And on the last day of the honeymoon cruise, some of *Britannia's* crew caught a three metre shark not far from the island in the Red Sea where the couple had gone swimming!

On the royal yacht – the dining room (top right)
the sun lounge (bottom right)

There was, too, one controversial note to the honeymoon. The couple's choice of Gibraltar for the start of *Britannia's* cruise obliged the King and Queen of Spain, whose country has long claimed the Rock of Gibraltar, to refuse their wedding invitation. Political wrangles were totally forgotten though when the Prince and Princess arrived in Gibraltar to a tumultuous and patriotic welcome. The royal pair drove along the three kilometre route from the airport to the dockyard to be greeted with cheers, confetti and even with faces painted Union Jack red, white and blue. While Charles and Diana watched and waved from the sun deck, many small craft followed as *Britannia* set sail on the latest of the many royal honeymoons the 4,900 tonne yacht has seen during her twenty-seven years in royal service.

On the royal yacht – the drawing room

An unguarded moment . . .

With her crew of 277 and her own Royal Marines band, *Britannia* is like a floating hotel. The royal apartments include a sun lounge, two studies and a spacious drawing room with grand piano, and plenty of floor space for dancing. Some of the furniture comes from *Britannia's* predecessor, the royal yacht *Victoria and Albert*, and the general style and décor reflect the taste of the Queen and the Duke of Edinburgh. Both took a personal interest in the fitting out of *Britannia* after she was launched by the Queen in Coronation year, 1953.

During the sun-soaked honeymoon fortnight, *Britannia* cruised through the Mediterranean, called briefly at Ithaca and Rhodes, then made her way down to the Red Sea, where the royal couple went snorkelling and diving.

At the Red Sea port of Hurghada

President Sadat and Prince Charles

The Princess with Mrs Sadat

On 15th August, Charles and Diana flew home from the remote Egyptian airfield of Hurghada. The Sadats were there to see them off and perhaps repeat the invitation extended at the dinner on board *Britannia* – to come back and see 'the delights of Egypt'. A few hours later, suntanned several shades browner than when they had left, the royal couple disembarked from their RAF VC-10 at Lossiemouth in the north of Scotland. From there, they went to Balmoral to join the rest of the royal family on their annual summer break in the Scottish Highlands, which Diana regards as one of the most beautiful places in the world.

Together again after Charles's Australian tour – relaxing at Balmoral in May

By long established understanding, the royals are left alone and uninterrupted during their holidays. So Charles and Diana once again disappeared from the curious public eye to enjoy another six weeks alone together, as they contemplated the public duties they were to undertake from the end of October. Nevertheless, the Prince and Princess did agree to meet the

After a walk with the dog (he's called Harvey)

The royals go shopping – Princess Margaret and the Princess of Wales in Ballater

Press on the banks of the River Dee, where they arrived suitably clad for a cool, wet summer day – Charles in kilt and sweater, Diana in country tweeds. The photographers were quick to notice the difference marriage had already made: Diana was more relaxed and self-assured in front of their cameras and had ready answers for questions about how she found married life. 'I can recommend it!' she commented.

There was also one public appearance, apart from Sunday morning visits to Crathie Kirk. In September, the Princess accompanied her husband and other members of the royal family to the Braemar Games where she emerged from the royal limousine clad in a Scots plaid outfit and black tam o' shanter.

At the Braemar Games

A tearful farewell

A faraway tragedy, which nevertheless affected Charles and Diana personally, interrupted the royal honeymoon when President Anwar Sadat of Egypt, so recently their host and guest, was assassinated during a military parade on 6th October. Charles had to leave Diana behind in England when he flew to Cairo to attend the funeral as the Queen's official representative.

There was a tearful farewell at the airport as the Princess, looking worried and upset, came to see Charles leave. It was reported that she wanted to accompany her husband, but the violent circumstances of Sadat's death, and the unrest and tension of Egypt after it, meant that security at the funeral was fraught with possible danger. So Diana had to stay behind. Despite difficulties and fears, however, Charles returned to his bride after only three days apart.

Prince Charles at President Sadat's funeral

Highgrove

The Prince and Princess of Wales have two homes of their own: an apartment in Kensington Palace when they need a London base for official engagements, and their country home in the Cotswolds, Highgrove House near Tetbury in Gloucestershire.

Highgrove House, which cost £800,000, was purchased for Prince Charles in the summer of 1980. The couple have royal neighbours – Princess Anne and Captain Mark Phillips, for instance, live at Gatcombe Park, not very far away. Built in rather plain Georgian style, Highgrove has nine main bedrooms, six bathrooms, and a nursery wing. It also has stables, adjoining farm buildings and extensive, elegant gardens.

At Kensington Palace *(shown above),* a royal residence since 1689, Charles and Diana have plenty of close relations as neighbours. Princess Margaret, Prince and Princess Michael of Kent, Princess Alice of Gloucester, and the Duke and Duchess of Gloucester all have apartments there. The Wales' apartments, consisting of four reception rooms, a master bedroom suite, a nursery suite and rooms for staff, have only recently been restored after suffering serious bomb damage during the Second World War.

As the newest member of what Charles once called 'the family firm', it was appropriate that his wife's first official engagement as Princess should be a tour of the Principality of Wales. It was a 'meet the people' tour, and despite forty-eight hours of pouring rain and biting autumn winds, Diana was determined to do just that. She plunged into the walkabouts with vigour, shaking hands until her own was red and sore, and frequently stopping for a few words with people in the huge crowds which gathered to greet her.

The Welsh tour . . .

The tour took the Prince and Princess from north to south, starting at the seaside resort of Rhyl, then on to Caernarvon Castle, where Prince Charles (then aged twenty), was presented to the Welsh people by the Queen in 1969. Now, it was Charles's turn to do the presenting!

Next day, 28th October, it was on to West Wales and St David's Cathedral to attend the Cathedral's 800th anniversary service. On 29th October, the last day of the tour, the royal couple were in Cardiff where they visited a maternity hospital. Diana received the Freedom of the City, an honour which she acknowledged with a short speech in Welsh.

4th November, the day the Queen opened the new Session of Parliament, was the day the Princess of Wales attended her first State ceremony. By tradition a splendid full-dress affair, Diana 'glittered from head to foot', as one admiring reporter described her. The Princess travelled from Buckingham Palace to Westminster in the same famous glass coach which had taken her to her wedding in July. Wearing white furs, a tiara and one of her favourite pearl choker necklaces, she sat next to her sister-in-law Princess Anne, and smiled and waved to the crowds all the way to Westminster.

She was still wearing the pearl choker that evening when she accompanied Prince Charles to the Victoria and Albert Museum in Kensington, for the inauguration of the 'Splendours of Gonzaga' Exhibition. The Princess arrived wearing a shimmering off-the-shoulder evening gown with cummerbund and bow at the waist, and another enthusiastic reporter called her 'enchantingly pretty'.

The State Opening of Parliament

'It was quite ridiculous,' said Earl Spencer, father of the Princess of Wales, 'to think that Diana could wait a year before starting a family.'

That was on 5th November – the day Buckingham Palace announced the glad news that the Princess who so adored children was expecting her first baby in June 1982. She was to become the youngest royal mother of the century.

As soon as the news was made public at 11 am that day, the congratulations began pouring in, and at a luncheon which the Prince and Princess attended at the Guildhall, the Lord Mayor of London was able to express personally the capital's pleasure.

Now attention was drawn to the colours of the newly-decorated nursery suite at Highgrove – blue and gold – and on the fact that 'boy first' had been the trend among royal couples ever since the Queen, as Princess Elizabeth, gave birth to Prince Charles in 1948. There was also the entertaining possibility that the Princess of Wales might have twins (a not infrequent occurrence in her own family). Whether boy or girl, the Royal Family's new member in 1982 will be second in line to the throne, after Prince Charles, and will take, from him, the title of Prince or Princess of Wales.

The expected baby meant, of course, curtailment of plans tentatively made for the Prince and Princess of Wales to tour countries in the British Commonwealth during 1982. But it also curtailed the Princess's activities at home, for morning sickness obliged her to cancel several engagements in November and December.

Arriving at the Guildhall

At York

'You've all got wives. You know the problems!' Prince Charles remarked philosophically to his tenants when he toured his Duchy of Cornwall alone instead of with his wife, as planned.

The chief problem seemed to be the strenuous all-day affair, when the Princess was in the public eye for hours on end. Sensibly, Diana decided it would be better to stick to short engagements instead.

At Chesterfield

At Chesterfield

One of the longer tours which she did fulfil, though, was a visit with Prince Charles to York and Chesterfield on 12th November. At York, the royal pair spent ninety minutes climbing in and out of the trains at the National Railway Museum, and afterwards took a short ride in a reproduction carriage of the Liverpool and Manchester Railway, hauled by a model of the famous Stephenson locomotive 'Rocket'. They followed this up with a drive round York Rugby Stadium in a Land Rover, while seven thousand school children waved and cheered from the terraces.

Then it was next stop Chesterfield, with Prince Charles himself piloting the helicopter for the short flight.

Elegant in velvet . . .

At Chesterfield, there was a seventeen million pound shopping precinct awaiting a royal opening, as well as a new three million pound police headquarters. Afterwards, the Prince and Princess attended a Thanksgiving Service at the 'crooked spire' parish church in Chesterfield.

Throughout the day, the Princess received good wishes galore and was handed dozens of bouquets, toys, and baby clothes.

Regent Street Christmas lights

Planting a commemorative tree at the Royal Thames Yacht Club

Another engagement Diana was determined not to miss was her first solo appearance. 'I left my old man at home watching the telly!' she said as she arrived in a midnight blue velvet suit to switch on the Regent Street Christmas lights on 18th November. She did rather better than her father, Earl Spencer, who on 24th November received an electric shock as he switched on Northampton's £20,000 Christmas lights!

Opening the Head Post Office at Northampton

Northampton, near the Spencer family home at Althorp, was the scene of the Princess's second solo engagement on 20th November. She opened a seven and a half million pound Head Post Office there. An enthusiastic, cheering crowd of ten thousand greeted her at Northampton, among them several hundred children enjoying a half day off school for the event.

At St Mary's Junior School, Tetbury

Clad for the cold – at Gloucester Cathedral

The first week in December found Charles and Diana at home in Gloucestershire, where they entertained Diana's elder sister, Lady Sarah, and several of their friends during their first stay of any length at Highgrove House. On 6th December, the Prince and Princess were at the parish church in nearby Tetbury for a concert in aid of the Benjamin Britten Fund for young musicians. Afterwards, the Princess was presented with a porcelain replica of her wedding bouquet: the real bouquet had, at her own request, been placed on the Tomb of the Unknown Soldier in London after the ceremony on 29th July.

The Princess went to Tetbury again on 8th December, driving her own car through the winter snow to visit the children of St Mary's Junior School.

Leaving the Royal Opera House, Covent Garden

At Guildford Cathedral

Cutting a Christmas cake

One fact was very much in evidence during the public engagements undertaken by the Princess of Wales in the first months of her marriage. The best chance of attention and a few words from Diana went automatically to the under-fives, her favourite age group! The Princess has, in fact, paid three visits to the kindergarten in Pimlico since she left her job there, and there was no shortage of youngsters at her first royal Christmas at Windsor in 1981. There were no fewer than six under-fives, two of them seven month old babies – Princess Anne's daughter Zara and Princess Michael's Gabriella.

For many years, Prince Charles has helped his parents fill the Christmas stockings for the youngest royals, and in 1981, Diana was there to join in. Her first royal Christmas also meant for Diana what she called the 'largest list I have ever drawn up', and she managed to do most of the shopping herself for gifts to her new family and her own, as well as to her staff and friends. And as Diana's first royal year drew to its close, there was 1982 and her own new baby to look forward to.

Christmas Day with the Royal family

The Direct Line of Succession

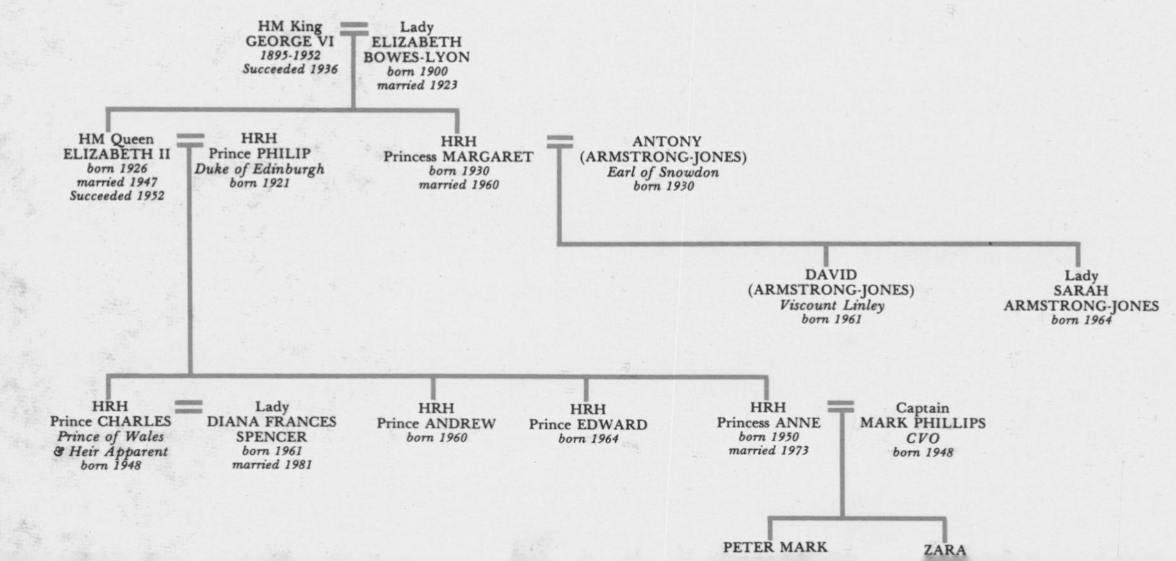